How t ]

People:

Effective Communication Skills To
Handle Difficult People.

A **How-To Guide** for Practicing the
Empathic Listening, Non-Verbal
Communication To Achieve
Relationship Success.

Wallace Ermes

TABLE OF CONTENTS

Introduction

I would like to thank you for purchasing this copy of my book. I would also like to extend to you a short congratulation for taking the first steps on the path to improving your communication skills and your ability to keep better conversations that can be more dynamic and organic.

The best place to start when trying to improve your communication skills is to go understand what communication actually is. This will help you to know what you should actually be focusing on and which skills you will want to work on a little bit more than whichever others, and how you can determine which areas you should be focusing on.

With all of that said, Communication can be described as the process by which two or more separate parties or individuals reach a mutual understanding, in which each participant not only exchange information, news, concepts, and feelings but also create and share the meanings behind them. In short, communication is a means of connection between or among people or places. Communication and the ability to communicate effectively are essential aspects of any sort of social interaction between or among people or parties, of both personal and professional nature.

"How to Raise Successful People: Effective Communication Skills To Handle Difficult People" is designed to help you to do just that; improve your conversations and communication skills as effectively as possible by focusing on the essential skills that you will need in order to effectively navigate your way through any and all social encounters you might experience. This book will focus on important skills that you can master and use in your daily life, starting with the type of mentality that you will need for effective communication and how you can put yourself in the right frame of mind for you. After that has been covered, the book will move on to the rest of its first section, which will be about 10 skills that are necessary for effective communication. Including the proper mentality, the chapters in this section will be listed below;

- Mentality. This chapter will focus on the best mindset to have for effective communication and why it can be important to be open-minded and have a good attitude and outlook, as well as how you can put yourself in a good emotional state for communicative purposes that are ideally also healthy for you as an individual.
- Active listening. This chapter will be focused on "active listening" and expressing interest when others are talking, as well as why this can also be important for effective communication on your end.

- Non-verbal Communication. This chapter will be about reading sub textual forms of indirect communication, such as gestures, facial expressions, and what people actually mean when they say different things, as well as why this can be helpful for effective communication.
- Clarity. This chapter will be centered on the concept of clarification and why it can be important to be clear and concise, as well as the importance of specificity when trying to convey concepts and ideas to other people.
- Imagery. This chapter will be somewhat of an extension of the last one and will expand on the concept of clarification to include indirect "imagery" like metaphors and other verbal techniques to convey concepts and ideas to others.
- Empathy. This chapter will focus on the concept of empathy, how it differs from sympathy, and why one (empathy) is better applied in situations that require clear and effective communication.
- Honesty. This chapter will be fairly straightforward, discussing the concept of honesty. Specifically, it will be about saying what you are thinking and being direct, as opposed to simply "not lying," as well as why it can be important to be direct when communicating with others.
- Respect. This chapter will focus on the concept of respect for others and their boundaries or preferences, as well as acceptance of those aspects and building trust.

- Criticism. This chapter will be centered on how to gracefully accept criticism, as well as offering it, as well as the meaning of constructive criticism and the concept behind the term, "Lashon hara," how they can affect the way you communicate with others, and why this can be important to effective communication.
- Confidence. This final chapter will focus on the idea of confidence, and delve deeper into that concept, covering related topics such as faith, acceptance of yourself and your environment, and the importance of humility.

After these 10 chapters have been finished, the book will then move on to its second section. Section 2 is called "5 Barriers to Effective Communication", and naturally, will discuss 5 topics that can act as barriers to effective communication. There will be a short introduction to the section and then jump into the 5 topics that will be included within the section, which will be listed below:

- Eye Contact. This chapter will discuss the importance of maintaining eye contact and why neglecting this aspect of communication can be detrimental, as well as how to do so effectively.
- Emotional States. This chapter will be focused on various emotional states and how they can affect the way you communicate with others, as well as how to escape from a negative emotional state or find positive ones.
- Mannerisms. This chapter will be focused on the ways you express yourself and how different

mannerisms and forms of expression can act as boundaries or barriers to effective communication.
- Enthusiasm. This chapter will cover the importance of enthusiasm and expressiveness in communicating effectively with others.
- Judgment. This chapter will be about judgment and how it differs from criticism, as well as how it can prevent effective communication between or among people.

Once you have gone through these two sections and their 15 chapters in this book, you should have all of the tools necessary to maximize your potential in social situations and learn how to communicate effectively with other people.

Section 1: Ten Skills to Help You Improve Your Communication

This first section of this book will be called "Ten Skills to Help You Improve Your Communication", and will cover 10 of the most essential skills that will be absolutely necessary to learn in order to communicate with other people and groups of people as effectively and efficiently as is possible. These skills are applicable in any and all social encounters that one might find themselves in. They can also be used in conjunction with one or more, or even all of the other skills that are included and discussed in this section of the book. Each of these skills can absolutely be applied alone, and every skill in this section, and the rest of the book as well, will each help you in social encounters and in communicating well with other people or groups.

Each separate topic in this book is designed to help you communicate more effectively with other people and will help you with this goal in the ways that are specific to each individual topic. They will also, however, work well with each of the other topics from their own respective chapters. While all of the skills in this book are designed to help you communicate effectively with others on their own, they can prove to be much more effective when used in combination with all of the other skills that are discussed and explained in this book. For example, the skill from the sixth chapter is referred to as "empathy." This can be applied on its own to any social encounter and will help you to communicate more effectively if applied. Empathy is a valuable skill to develop, of course. However, it is also a very useful and versatile skill. The ability to understand and even share the feelings of another person, and even to put yourself in that person's shoes, can be helpful in developing many of the later skills that are covered in this first section of this book. It is much easier to find respect for a person or group and to build trust with them if you can understand their point of view and how they may be feeling in a given moment in time.

Additionally, this section as a whole has been designed to naturally flow from one skill to the next in a way that will feel organic and will allow for you to understand the concepts that are covered in each individual chapter as easily as possible. Many of the chapters in this section and the concepts and ideas contained within them build on those that are included in previous chapters or are meant to set up for those that will be included in later chapters. The first chapter of this section, for example, is about the mentality and mindset that will best suit the goal of improving your communication skills and the importance of keeping a positive mindset in order to accomplish this goal. The final chapter of the section is called "confidence" and will be best applied with the information from the first chapter kept in mind. A very large point of focus within this chapter will be the concept of humility and its importance for effective communication. This will, of course, be more effective when approached with the proper state of mind for the maximum amount of effectiveness. The chapters on the concepts of clarity and imagery will also work especially well together as well. The fourth chapter of this section is called "Clarity" and will focus primarily on the importance of being as clear and concise as possible. A very large portion of this chapter will be about this concept of the importance of clear communication, and how to accurately explain various topics to other people by explaining these concepts with specificity. The fifth chapter, which is called "Imagery," will then immediately build on that idea and expand upon it by further explaining the importance of clear communication and helping other people or groups to understand the points that you intend to share with them. It will then explain that an incredibly effective method for doing this is to use expressive and indirect imagery that those individuals or parties will be able to relate to much more easily, in order to more accurately convey the concepts and ideas that you are attempting to share with those people or groups.

Each of these chapters has been designed to work well with and build off of the previous chapters in a way that flows organically with all of the others in the section, as stated previously. While it is not advised to read these chapters out of order, it is definitely possible. For instance, you may find yourself finishing one chapter and wishing to circle back to another chapter that was covered previously, or even jumping forward to a future chapter and coming back afterward. While this is, as was stated previously, not advised, you may wish to plan your own way through the contents of this book. In the event that this is the case, the chapters in this section will be listed below once again:

- Mentality. This chapter will focus on the best mindset to have for effective communication and why it can be important to be open-minded and have a good attitude and outlook, as well as how you can put yourself in a good emotional state for communicative purposes that are ideally also healthy for you as an individual.
- Active listening. This chapter will be focused on "active listening" and expressing interest when others are talking, as well as why this can also be important for effective communication on your end.
- Non-verbal Communication. This chapter will be about reading sub textual forms of indirect communication, such as gestures, facial expressions, and what people actually mean when they say different things, as well as why this can be helpful for effective communication.
- Clarity. This chapter will be centered on the concept of clarification and why it can be important to be clear and concise, as well as the

importance of specificity when trying to convey concepts and ideas to other people.

- Imagery. This chapter will be somewhat of an extension of the last one and will expand on the concept of clarification to include indirect "imagery" like metaphors and other verbal techniques to convey concepts and ideas to others.
- Empathy. This chapter will focus on the concept of empathy, how it differs from sympathy, and why one (empathy) is better applied in situations that require clear and effective communication.
- Honesty. This chapter will be fairly straightforward, discussing the concept of honesty. Specifically, it will be about saying what you are thinking and being direct, as opposed to simply "not lying," as well as why it can be important to be direct when communicating with others.
- Respect. This chapter will focus on the concept of respect for others and their boundaries or preferences, as well as acceptance of those aspects and building trust.
- Criticism. This chapter will be centered on how to gracefully accept criticism, as well as offering it, as well as the meaning of constructive criticism and the concept behind the term, "Lashon hara," how they can affect the way you communicate with others, and why this can be important to effective communication.
- Confidence. This final chapter will focus on the idea of confidence, and delve deeper into that concept, covering related topics such as faith,

acceptance of yourself and your environment, and the importance of humility.

Chapter 1: Mentality

The first point that will help you to on the road to improving your conversational skills and in learning how to communicate with other people and groups of people much more effectively is a basic one. This chapter will be focused on the concept of mentality. This chapter will go over various topics related to the concept of mentality. The first part of this chapter will be about the importance of a person's state of mind with regards to when they are trying to communicate with others and how different mental states can affect the different ways in which people can convey the ideas and concepts that they want to convey, and even how they can affect the effectiveness of that communication. This chapter will also explain topics similar and related to mentality as it relates to this book's theme of effective communication, such as your outlook toward other people and the world around you, and the importance of keeping an open mind and being accepting of various situations (especially negative ones) as well as how to actually do so. Once you have completed this chapter, you should have all of the tools necessary to master the skills that will be covered in each of the remaining chapters in this section of the book, as well as all of the chapters to be covered in the second section as well.

The first, and arguably most important skill that will be covered in this section will be referred to as "mentality." In this context, the term "mind" is used to describe the mindset that you carry, your attitudes about yourself, others, and the world around you, and your particular way of thinking in relation to a person or group. This can be incredibly important when trying to improve your communication skills, as an especially negative mindset can cloud your judgment, or even affect the way you act and how effectively you can communicate. For example, if you happen to be having a bad day or are maybe a little irritated or upset, and someone approaches you to ask a question about work or asks you for advice on something that might be important to them, you might turn them away or even lash out and act rudely. With a positive state of mind, most people would handle this situation much differently, and in most cases, much more effectively. A person who is in a more positive state of mind might react to this situation in a manner that is much more helpful for the other person and themselves, like providing an answer that they think will help the other person or even relating to that person and connecting with them in a way that helps them to understand what they need to do on their own, teaching them how to figure it out on their own rather than simply receiving the answer without any explanation. Sometimes, however, people don't necessarily want advice. Instead, they might want to verify or receive validation for a decision that they've made. If they are looking for validation, it might be because they are thinking about possibly making a decision that could be unhealthy or harmful to themselves and want or needs to be told that this might be the case. In these situations, a positive and constructive state of mind can also make the difference between wildly different outcomes. Knowing how to approach a topic such as telling someone that they might be wrong or making the wrong choice can be somewhat difficult. If handled poorly, these types of issues can even result in some sort of conflict or argument and can escalate very quickly. This will also be important during the chapters on active listening, clarity, empathy, honesty, and respect. As for this current chapter's topic, there are many different ways that you can know what types of mental states work best for you and how to put yourself in a good frame of mind that works for you or even pull yourself out of a bad one that might not help you so much.

The easiest way to understand the topic of mindsets is with the context of a challenging situation. When you are faced with a challenging situation or a difficult choice that might be outside of your personal comfort zone, you are automatically presented with a choice. In these situations, you are always able to choose between two options. These options can be described as two very different and directly opposing types of mindsets; The Fixed mindset, which typically, as the name would imply, fixed. A person with a "fixed" mindset will typically act in ways that can often prevent development in favor of comfort. This can cause a person's growth to sort of plateau and remain static, or "fixed. For many people, this state of mind can be a result of a strong desire or even an obsession on appearances or insecurity. This can lead a person to avoid challenging situations, to view difficulty as fruitless and give up very easily, to disregard helpful feedback and criticism, and to feel threatened by the success of others. On the other end of the spectrum is the fixed mindset's direct opposite, referred to as the "Growth mindset." A person who has a mindset focused on growth will normally go out of their way to make active decisions that will benefit themselves and others in the long term and will allow them to, as the name would suggest, grow and develop as people. This growth-centric state of mind is, as the opposite to the fixed mindset, a result of the active decision and difficult choices that need to be kept in mind, as well as a willingness and eagerness to learn from mistakes and successes in order to continue to grow. Maintaining a "growth mindset" will require you to keep your options in mind in order to recognize and choose the path that will help you to develop and continue to improve as a person. A person with a growth mindset will actively choose to embrace challenging or difficult situations, remain persistent and determined under stress, choose to view adversity as a path or step to success and self-improvement, accept and learn from criticism gracefully, and be inspired and motivated by other people's successes. These two opposing mindsets can be separated by five main points, all related to how they choose to handle various situations, especially difficult ones. These differences are listed below:

- Challenges. The first difference that can be found between these two mindsets is how the people who carry them tend to react to challenging situations. The "fixed mindset" individual will typically shy away from challenges in an effort to avoid failure. This is usually strongly connected to a sense of insecurity. A person with a "growth mindset" will usually embrace these types of challenges as opportunities for growth and development.

- Adversity. When a "Fixed Mindset" personality is faced with adversity, they will tend to give up very easily. This is directly opposed to people with a "growth mindset," who will choose instead to remain determined when faced with adversity and setbacks in order to accomplish their goals.

- Effort. A person with a "fixed mindset" will typically carry a sense of nihilism, and will view effort and strife as meaningless. An individual who focuses more on personal growth will instead choose to view difficulty as a vehicle that will carry them to success.

- Criticism. An individual with a "fixed mindset" will tend to view criticism as hostility as a result of a sense of insecurity and will disregard or reject criticism in many cases, whereas a growth-focused person will accept criticism and use it to develop and grow as a person.

- The success of other people. A person who is focused on appearances and has a fixed mindset will normally feel threatened by the success of people around them, and even insecure about their own lack of success. An individual who focuses on growth and development, on the other hand, will be accepting of their peers' success and take the opportunity to learn and find motivation.

Additionally, there are a few very easy ways that you can use to change your mindset, and that can help you become a much more well-adjusted person. There are ways to develop the "growth mindset" that will allow you to develop and maximize your potential as a person and that will give you the tools necessary to deal with the remaining chapters in this section as well as the rest of this book as a whole. The way to do so is to make active decisions focusing on the concept of growth, and the steps necessary in order to do this are listed below:

- Learn to perceive your mindset as a voice in your mind. Your mindset controls the ways that you talk to yourself and the ways that you think to yourself. The first step on the way to developing a growth mindset is to realize this fact and learn to recognize this "voice" as it speaks to you. When you are faced with a challenging or difficult situation, this voice might tell you that you aren't capable of success in that situation, or that you will fail and even trying is pointless. Paying attention to these thoughts as they occur can help you to recognize any patterns or thoughts that you experience frequently. Once you realize these thoughts, you can begin to put an end to them and move on to a more constructive and healthy state of mind.

- Choose growth. Once you've learned to recognize your "internal voice" and how it can manifest within your mind, you can choose to move past your doubts and negative thoughts. At this point, you can move forward by acknowledging that you aren't stuck with those thoughts, doubts, and insecurities. You are capable of moving past those thoughts, doubts, and insecurities, and you can actively decide how you will choose to handle any challenges, criticism, or obstacles that you encounter. This does, however, require action and constant attention, and can be difficult to maintain at times.

- Argue. When you experience negative thoughts or doubts in the form of your "inner voice," you can choose to "talk back" to that voice. You should try to be as critical of it as you can, as well. Tell it exactly what is wrong with how it frames these situations and actively reshape your mentality with regards to these challenging situations to reflect a focus on personal improvement and growth.

Act. The final step in this progression is to use the previous steps, and the information you gained from them would be to act on your newly realized growth mentality. The point of developing a growth mentality is not only to affect your thoughts but your actions too. Maintaining a "growth mindset" is about active decisions that need to be kept in mind as much and as often as possible.

Smile. This one is a very simple concept. Simply smiling and keeping a light attitude can help a lot in a tense or difficult situation. Of course, it is very important to know the right situations to use this skill in, but if you keep the context of the situation in mind, simply being able to laugh and smile in the face of adversity is a very valuable skill to master. A smile can become a very powerful tool if it is used correctly. A warm and genuine smile can often help a quiet or reserved individual feel more comfortable and more willing to talk to you, for example.

This can be very helpful for easing a nervous or uncomfortable person into a more positive state of mind. Being able to maintain a positive attitude in difficult situations can be an incredibly useful tool for improving your communication skills.

Chapter 2: Active Listening

The next point that will help you to on the road to improving your conversational skills and in learning how to communicate with other people and groups of people much more effectively is another simple one. This chapter will be focused on the concept of "active listening." This chapter will go over various topics related to the concept of active listening, as well. The first part of this chapter will be about the importance of showing interest and expressing that you are listening to another person trying to talk to you with regards to when they are trying to communicate with others and how having the ability to listen "actively" to other people can affect the different ways in which people can convey the ideas and concepts that they want to convey, and even how they can affect the effectiveness of that communication. This chapter will also explain topics similar and related to active listening as it relates to this book's theme of effective communication, such as how people will perceive and react to the way or ways that you handle yourself in listening to other people attempting to communicate with you, as well as how to actually do so. Once you've completed this chapter, you should have all of the tools necessary to master the skills that will be covered in each of the remaining chapters in this section of the book, as well as all of the chapters to be covered in the second section as well.

The second very important skill that will be covered in this section will be referred to as "active listening." In this context, the term "active listening" will be used to describe a specific way of listening to others and the concepts or ideas that they may be attempting to communicate with or to you, and responding or reacting to them in ways that create or strengthen a mutual understanding between you. This can be incredibly important when you are trying to improve your communication skills, as the ability to maintain effective communication with other people consists of both speaking and listening to those people. Active listening can be an excellent first step to defusing a hostile situation or even affect the way or ways that you act and how effectively you can communicate with that person. For example, if we use the same example as in the first chapter, wherein you might be experiencing a particularly bad or unpleasant day, or you are maybe a little bit irritated or upset, and someone approaches you to ask a question about work or asks you for advice on something that might be important to them, we can get a clear image of how this skill of active listening can help you communicate effectively with others.

The concept of simply "Listening good" may seem unimportant or even counterintuitive to our overarching

goal of learning how to communicate
especially if you consider that by simply
people talk to you, you are acting in an alm
counterintuitive capacity to this concept by ta
opposite stance and receiving the concepts and
another person is communicating to you. If you h
be having a bad day or are maybe a little irritated or
upset, and someone approaches you to ask a question
about work or asks you for advice on something that
might be important to them, how you choose to handle
this situation can affect the outcome. You might turn
them away or act rudely, which can cause them to leave
you alone at that moment as you might prefer, but it will
also prevent them from coming to you in the future with
any difficult or sensitive topics that they might need help
with. This can also result in that person being less willing
to talk to you and listen to what you might have to say in
the future as well, especially if this situation is handled
especially poorly. A person who feels validated and
listened to will be much more willing to listen to you as
well.

Active listening is a skill that is all about understanding
another individual or group of people and building trust
by building a rapport and allowing the people who you
are attempting to "Actively listen to" to feel heard and
respected. In learning and mastering the skills that are
listed below, you can learn to be a more effective listener,
to hear people more effectively, and to let them know that
you are hearing and understanding the concepts and ideas
that they are trying to communicate to you. This is a
proven psychological skill that can help you to
communicate your own ideas with other people. It can
also help the other person to not only feel heard and

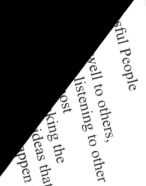

ıfortable with their
llow them to more
and ideas that are
ish to convey to you and
ːveral methods that you
ɔw people that you are
ˈhich will be listed

...ow the person who you
... ʊ ɪnat you are listening to them, a
ɡood technique to use is to periodically repeat what that person is saying, as you understand it, in order to verify their meaning.

- Summarization. This is another method of clarification that can help you in showing interest in what another person is saying to you. A more active alternative to repetition, summarization involves bringing the facts and pieces of another person's words together in your own words in order to verify that you understand and reassure them that you are listening.

- Encouragement. You can use short words of encouragement to help keep a conversation going and to show that you are paying attention and want to know more. Things like nods or asking what happened next when someone is telling a story would fall under this category.

- Reflection. You can also use "reflection" to give feedback when someone is talking to you by stepping in their shoes and attempting to understand their feelings about the situation and sort of mirror them, displaying a sense of empathy.

- Feedback. Letting people know what you think about a situation can be another way of letting them know that you are interested in what they have to say. You can share relevant information with them as well as any observations, insights, or relevant experiences that might help them.
- Emotion labeling. If you discuss a person's feelings or emotions with them, it can sometimes help that person to see their situation from another perspective, usually a more objective one.
- Probe. A good way to instill confidence and reassure a person that you understand what they are attempting to communicate with you is to simply ask questions about the topic to get deeper or more meaningful information.
- Validation. A good way to show someone that you are listening is through validation. Many times when people are talking about a stressful subject or situation, they simply want to feel validated. If you acknowledge the person's issues and their feelings, this will help them out and will reassure them that you care about their feelings and emotions, which will build trust between you.
- Silence. This might seem counterproductive based on the information within the rest of this chapter, but sometimes a comfortable silence can slow down a conversation and allow all parties to calm down and assess the situation.
- "I" speech. You've most likely heard this one before. By using "I" in your statements, it makes it easier to focus more on the situation as opposed to the person. It can also help you to convey ideas more effectively to the recipient.

Chapter 3: Non-verbal Communication

The next point that will help you to on the road to improving your conversational skills and in learning how to communicate with other people and groups of people much more effectively is another simple one. This chapter will be focused on the concept of "non-verbal communication." This chapter will go over various topics related to the concept of non-verbal communication, as well. The first part of this chapter will be about the importance of using non-verbal communication techniques and "body language" in order to help you to convey various concepts, ideas, or feelings. with regards to when they are trying to communicate with others and how having the ability to use things like gestures, tone, posture, and other forms of expression can affect the different ways in which people can convey the ideas and concepts that they are wanting to convey, and even how they can affect the effectiveness of that communication. This chapter will also explain topics similar and related to nonverbal communication as it relates to this book's theme of effective communication, such as what nonverbal communication is, why it can be an important aspect of effective communication as well as how to actually do so. Once you've completed this chapter, you should have all of the tools necessary to master the skills that will be covered in each of the remaining chapters in this section of the book, as well as all of the chapters to be covered in the second section as well.

The next very important skill that will be covered in this will be called "nonverbal communication." In this context, the term "nonverbal communication" is used to describe various ways that you can use to communicate ideas or feelings with or to other people or groups without using actual words, such as body language, posture, tone, facial expressions, gestures, and eye contact (or the lack of eye contact in some cases) and other ways in which people are able to communicate with others without necessarily using words. This can be incredibly important when trying to improve your communication skills, as the ability to communicate in this way can help you convey the right feelings or emotions, or help to inform a person or group of people about your stance on a particular topic. Your tone, posture, or facial expressions can give these people various clues as to how YOU feel about what you are talking about, or even about them. On the other hand, however, if you are not paying attention to these aspects of communication, they can even be detrimental to effective communication. If you are attempting to verbally express a positive opinion on a particular subject or topic while also simultaneously holding a negative expression on your face or a hostile tone, this can portray a sort of dissonance between your words and actions. This can be counterproductive to your goals, as "actions speak louder than words." Many people might even interpret your tone or expressions as being about them, as opposed to the subject you are discussing, as well. This can also be harmful to communication both in the present and future, as these negative feelings as they are perceived can act as an obstacle in this way. For example, if we use the same example as in the first chapter wherein you might be experiencing a particularly bad or unpleasant day, or are maybe a little bit irritated or upset and someone approaches you to ask a question about work or asks you for advice on something that might be important to them, we can get a clear image of how this skill of nonverbal communication can help you communicate more effectively with others.

In this scenario, a friend of yours comes to you with a question about work, or they want advice on a difficult and maybe somewhat sensitive issue that they are struggling with. Again, you have been having a particularly bad or unpleasant day and might feel a little bit irritated or upset when this friend approaches you. When they ask you about their problem or problems, you have a very negative expression on your face and use a somewhat hostile tone when you answer them. Maybe you are trying to move past your own mood and help this person, and you are genuinely offering advice that you think might be helpful to them, but you aren't paying as much attention to the nonverbal ways in which you communicate. As you try to help them, they notice the tone of your voice as you offer them this advice or they see your expression and might interpret these forms of nonverbal communication to be related to the topic you are discussing or even about them. When this happens, it can confuse the person and make them somewhat insecure or uncomfortable and can draw attention away from the advice that you are attempting to give them. For this reason, it can be incredibly important to keep this type of nonverbal communication in mind. In addition to simply remembering the importance of nonverbal communication, there are many ways that you can improve the ways that you communicate with other people in this way. These "nonverbal communication skills" will be listed below:

- Facial expressions. Facial expressions can play a very large role in nonverbal communication. This is the first thing that most people look at in terms of nonverbal forms of communication and is arguably the most important. Unlike some of the ways that people can communicate nonverbally, our facial expressions are mostly universal. The expressions of happiness, anger, sadness, and many other different emotions that are common between cultures are all the same between and across those cultures.
- Posture and movement. If you keep in mind how the ways that you perceive other people or groups of people are affected by the ways that they carry themselves when they are standing, walking, or sitting, the importance of this posture can become much clearer. The way that you carry yourself can convey a lot of information about yourself to other people. Crossing your arms is seen as a defensive stance, and slouching or holding yourself upright can tell a person how excited you are about a particular situation or topic.
- Gestures. Gestures can be a very important aspect of nonverbal communication as well. Much like your posture, these gestures can tell a person or a

group of people a lot about yourself and the way or ways that you feel about a particular situation or topic. Waving can indicate your level of excitement about meeting or seeing a person or a group of people, depending on the level of enthusiasm you use and the context of your wave. Shrugging can express to a person that you do not know the answer to a question or that you are confused by the topic. The "OK" hand sign of forming a circle with your thumb and index finger conveys a somewhat positive message in some cultures, but in others, it can be seen as offensive.

- Eye contact. This is a fairly obvious point and one that you probably would have heard at some point in the past. Similarly, and as an extension to the topic of facial expressions, eye contact can be a very important part of nonverbal communication. Eyes are the windows to the soul, as they say, and the way that you look at a person can communicate a lot of very different ideas, including things like your level of interest in the topic of the conversation or even about the person you are talking to. This can also be important and even vital to maintaining the flow of the conversation, and judging how the other person might be feeling about these topics as well.

- Touch. Another way that people can communicate to and with other individuals and groups is through physical contact. Establishing any sort of physical contact with another person can enforce a sort of closeness or a bond between or among people if done right and depending on the context. This can also be harmful if done wrong or under a poor context as well, however. A weak handshake or a person grabbing the arm of another person strongly as an act of control, for example, can have a very negative impact on the relationship between those two people.

- Space. This is also a very effective tool for effective communication. Different people or groups of people, depending on various factors such as the culture they come from, can feel very differently about the rules of "personal space." The concept of a "personal bubble" is fairly universal across all cultures, but some have very different stances on the subject. This can also be somewhat dependent on the relationship between two people or groups of people, as well. A romantic partner or close friend might be okay or even encourage more physical closeness with you than a stranger or work associate.

- Tone. The tone that you use when you are talking to other people or groups of people can have a large impact on the way that that person perceives your words or even assumes that you feel about a particular topic or even about them. This includes your level of enthusiasm or possibly an angry tone, and can even go down to the level of confidence that you convey in your words and using transitionary words or phrases such as "like," or "um" to pause and make rehearsed speech feel more organic.

- The "Silent Treatment." This form of non-verbal communication is a little bit different from the other ones that have been discussed in this chapter, as it is typically much more deliberate than any of the others. Usually, this "silent treatment" is used intentionally to send a message that a person is upset with you or doesn't feel like talking. Usually, people will refuse to speak to a particular individual, or even to a group of people. This can be one of the most effective strategies for communication, even if it seems a little bit unintuitive to avoid speaking in order to send a message. Additionally, depending on the context that it is used in, it can have very different meanings. If someone has done something wrong, giving them the "silent treatment" can let them know that you don't want to talk to them at the moment. You've probably seen many examples of this in various forms of media, like television or in books. Using this "silent treatment" can also be used in positive contexts, as well, however. If someone is telling a story or giving you information, remaining silent can be extremely effective in getting that person to share more information with you. In the case of a story that someone is telling you, you might typically wait until they have finished a statement and respond easily. If you instead choose to stay silent while still expressing that you are paying attention to them and listening to what they have to say, this can encourage that person to volunteer more information that they otherwise would have. In this case, staying silent will leave a gap in the conversation during which they will continue with their story or the point that they were making. In a situation where a person is angry or upset, they might be venting to you about various frustrations that they might have. If you simply let them continue expressing these strong feelings and emotions, it can help them to work through them, and can sometimes even be more effective than if you had asked about the situation and asked them to elaborate. This technique can also work similarly with people who are telling you a story or discussing something that they are enthusiastic or excited about, as well. Instead of having to encourage communication, this "silent treatment" can allow the conversation to continue naturally and on its own.

- Listening. This is arguably the most effective form of non-verbal communication. When you are communicating with another person or group of people, listening and making sure that they know they are being heard can be incredibly important. In many cases, communication can effectively become useless, or it can become difficult to maintain effective communication if you are not actively listening to and understanding what other people are saying to you. Effective communication is all about making sure that the people you are talking to feel heard and appreciated. If someone is responding to the things that you are saying, you should be actively trying to hear and understand those responses, and use that information to grow. If a person is giving you feedback on something you've done or said, then you should accept that feedback and change the way that you approach that situation in the future. Give people a platform to voice their concerns, and help them feel heard. If you listen to the things a person says to you, they might also be more willing to listen to your points in the future, as well.

Chapter 4: Clarity

The next point that will help you to on the road to improving your conversational skills and in learning how to communicate with other people and groups of people much more effectively is another simple one. This chapter will be focused on the concept of "clarity." This chapter will go over various topics related to the concept of clear communication, as well. The first part of this chapter will be about the importance of maintaining clarity when talking to other people or groups of people for effective communication, with regards to when they are trying to communicate with others and how having the ability to communicate clearly and accurately with other people or groups of people can affect the different ways in which people can convey the ideas and concepts that they want to convey, and even how they can affect the effectiveness of that communication. This chapter will also explain topics similar and related to speaking with clarity as it relates to this book's theme of effective communication, such as what it means to speak clearly and different things that can act as barriers to clarity when talking with others, as well as how to improve your communication skills with other people by learning how to speak more clearly. Once you've completed this chapter, you should have all of the tools necessary to master the skills that will be covered in each of the remaining chapters in this section of the book, as well as all of the chapters to be covered in the second section as well.

The next very important skill that will be covered in this section will be called "clarity." In this context, the term "clarity" is used to describe the ability or skill of being able to communicate the ideas and concepts that you are attempting to communicate with other people accurately and effectively. This skill can be an incredibly important aspect of attempting to improve your overall communication skills, as the ability to communicate in this way can help you to convey the right feelings or emotions, or to help to inform a person or group of people about your stance on a particular topic. Things like enunciation and specificity can help you to give these people a much easier time in understanding the concepts, ideas, feelings, and emotions that you might want to convey to them. On the other hand, however, these can be detrimental to the ways in which you can communicate with other people or groups of people if you are not paying proper attention to them and their application. It can also be important to understand different forms of communication and different media with which you can communicate with people, as well as the benefits and limitations of these various media. For example, attempting to communicate subjective matters such as feelings or opinions can be very difficult in any sort of text-based medium, such as through SMS text or email, due to the lack of many of the nonverbal forms of communication that are available when communicating with a person or group of people in person, such as facial expressions, gestures, and tone. Because of this fact, it can be very easy for the recipient to project emotions and opinions onto text-based communication based on their own assumptions, which can greatly affect the ways that a conversation can proceed. This can also be harmful to communication both in the present and future, as these negative feelings as they are perceived can act as an obstacle in this way. For example, if we use the same example as in the first chapter wherein you might be experiencing a particularly bad or unpleasant day, or are maybe a little bit irritated or upset and someone approaches you to ask a question about work or asks you for advice on something that might be important to them, we can get a clear image of how this skill of clear communication can help you communicate more effectively with others.

In this scenario, you have been having a particularly bad or unpleasant day and might feel a little bit irritated or upset when this friend approaches you. When they ask you about their problem or problems, you try to give them some advice that you genuinely believe will help them in this situation, but this advice happens to be sort of extreme or might need a little bit more information or explanation in order to make sense. Or maybe this friend of yours asks you for advice in a text message, and you respond to them with your feelings or opinions on the subject and they interpret your words as hostile. You didn't intend for this result, but it can be very difficult to convey tone through text when you don't have access to nonverbal forms of communication. For this reason, it can be incredibly important to keep this skill of speaking clearly in mind in order to maintain effective communication. In addition to simply remembering the importance of clear and accurate communication, there are many ways that you can improve the ways that you communicate with other people in this way. These "clearer communication skills" will be listed below:

Nonverbal Communication. This was covered in an earlier chapter, but can also be incredibly helpful to you for the purpose of maintaining clarity and guiding the way that the person or people who you are talking to will perceive your intention and attitude about the topic or topics that is or are being discussed. A number of studies have found that nonverbal communication accounts for a large majority of how an "audience" ended up perceiving a presenter or speaker.

Overcommunication. There was a study that was conducted in 1990 at Stanford University that proved that presenters and speakers typically overestimate how much their audience and listeners pay attention to and understand. The people involved in this study became known as the "tappers" and the "listeners." One group of participants was asked to tap the melody of various songs on a surface for the other participants, the "listeners" to guess at. The listeners would guess the rhythm that was being tapped. The tappers had guessed that about half of the songs that were to be guessed would be correctly identified. In reality, however, when the results had been calculated, only about 2.5 percent of the songs that were tapped had been identified correctly. This study can be extremely helpful in demonstrating the importance of clear communication and that in order for your thoughts and concepts to be understood properly, they need to be made as clear as possible, through "over-communication," especially for new or unfamiliar ideas. In most cases, listeners and audiences do not tend to absorb as much as the speaker would expect them to.

Avoid visual aids. This point might seem a little bit counterintuitive, but Steve Jobs of Apple, Inc. actually implemented a rule within the company that placed a pan on PowerPoint presentations and similar visual aids to his employees' presentations. Sheryl Sandberg also had a similar rule on Facebook. Both of these individuals had come to the realization that PowerPoint presentations and other types of visual aids can actually serve to hinder communication rather than to help it. You should instead use other techniques such as nonverbal communication and specificity in order to communicate your concepts and ideas.

Ask for feedback. This can be a good way to make sure that your "audience" understands the topic or topics that you are talking about, as well as to help them to understand the subject matter better by stating it themselves. This can also help you to find different ways that you can improve in your own communication that you might not have considered before such as gaps or points of confusion for the people listening to you.

Interact with your "audience." Regardless of the topics or the context all individuals have somewhat limited attention spans. In order to become a more effective conversationalist and learn to communicate more effectively, you should attempt to include other people and get their opini0ns of the matter. If you ask someone a question or encourage them to talk about their stances or opinions it can help them to pay attention more and to understand the topic a little bit better.

Focus on the beginning and the end. If you consider the attention span of yourself and of other people, it can become clear that sometimes it can be good to separate the information that you convey. Most of the time, people will remember the beginning and end of a lot of things much more accurately than in the middle. This can be difficult, as this makes up a large majority of most conversations and speeches, and holds the most important information. But if you reiterate important points in the beginning and end, it can help recipients of this information to absorb it better.

Chapter 5: Imagery

This chapter will be focusing on a skill very similar and related to the one from the last, and like the chapters before, the skill to be discussed in this chapter will be very helpful on the path to improving your conversational skills and in learning how to communicate more effectively with other people and groups of people. The actual topic to be discussed in this chapter is referred to as" imagery." Imagery, in this context, will be used to describe the use of various literary devices to help you to communicate important concepts, ideas, and points to other people in ways that they will understand. This chapter will also go over the importance of using this kind of imagery in order to accurately and effectively communicate various concepts and ideas to other people or groups of people, as well as how to improve your communication skills with other people by using this imagery in your speech to help with your communication with other people. Once you've completed this chapter, you should have all of the tools necessary to master the skills that will be covered in each of the remaining chapters in this section of the book, as well as all of the chapters to be covered in the second section as well.

The next very important skill that will be covered in this section will be very closely related to the topic of "clarity" from the previous chapter, and will be called "imagery." In this context, the term "imagery" is being used to describe the ability or skill of being able to use various literary devices in order to communicate the ideas and concepts that you are attempting to communicate with other people accurately and effectively, and in ways that they will be able to understand more easily. This can be an incredibly important aspect of your ability to communicate effectively overall, as the ability to convey various concepts and ideas to other people in ways that they will easily be able to understand can help people to understand you more easily, which will, in turn, help them to be more willing to talk and listen to you, improving the overall quality of your interactions with them.

In this chapter, I will list a number of various literary devices that can be useful for effective communication between or among different people. Along with each will be a definition of the term to explain it, as well as an explanation of why, how, and when each of these skills can be useful to you for effective communication and how to actually use these skills in your conversations with other people and groups of people.

These types of "literary devices" are techniques for communication that you can use to create specific effects in your speech to convey specific information or to help another person or group of people to understand your words on a deeper level and with much more ease. In most cases, these literary devices are used for emphasis or to enforce clarity in conversation. This is why these chapters have been placed together, as they are very closely connected. These skills can be used in order to help other people to relate or connect more strongly with your points and intentions in conversation. The various skills that will help you to do this and their explanations will be listed below:

Allegory: An allegory is a picture, poem, or story that can be used to represent an important meaning rooted in life by the association to real issues of important or relevant concepts or topics. This might take the form of a novel or a work of art, or in this case, a short story told to another person that parallels a relevant situation. This sort of story is typically used to suggest a specific path or action that one might think they or another person should take in their current situation.

Alliteration: an alliteration can be defined as a series of words or phrases that all (or most of which) begin with the same or very similar sounds. These common sounds are usually connected by or begin with consonants, in order to add more stress to that first syllable. The most common uses of alliteration are in poetry, titles, or short phrases to catch the attention of the "audience." This device usually has a similar effect to that of repetition, in that it can help to emphasize a point, but differs in the extent of this emphasis and the types of points they can emphasize. Repetition can enforce a larger point by "hammering in" a specific line of words, whereas alliteration will typically enforce the feeling of a certain phrase or the point that that phrase makes by repeating a specific sound and drawing attention to it.

Allusion can be defined as an indirect reference to any object, person, place, event, or concept that exists outside of the topic that is already being discussed, such as a book, film, or other work of art or literature. Most often, people will reference events or topics that relate to popular culture in order to compare a person, place, or event to another that they will be familiar with. Making this kind of association or connection can help a person to see your point of view about a thing or situation.

Anaphora: Anaphora is very similar to alliteration in that it involves repetition, but differs in the extent of this repetition. Anaphora involves the repetition of a specific word or phrase at the beginning of multiple sentences in order to emphasize the phrase that is being repeated and evoke strong feelings based on the repeated phrase in the "audience." A great example of the use of this device is the repetition of "We shall fight" in reference to the numerous places that the British army would continue to fight during the second world war, during Winston

Churchill's speech called "We Shall Fight on the Beaches." This was used to rally the British troops and people in order to instill in them the confidence in their nation and that they would win the war. This repeated use of the phrase "We will fight" helped to emphasize the fact that the British army would endure that difficult time and strengthen the impact of the speech as a whole.

Asyndeton: This is a slightly different term from the others that have been included so far. Asyndeton can be described as the intentional exclusion of certain conjunctions in a cluster of words or phrases so as to emphasize the meaning or impact of that sentence or phrase. This device is typically used in speeches or important discussions to give it a more powerful and memorable feel and rhythm.

Epistrophe: An epistrophe is very similar to the device of anaphora. It is similar in the use of a repeated word or phrase in multiple sentences but differs in that the repeated word or phrase typically appears at the end of slightly different statements. This type of repetition can be used, similarly to anaphora, to evoke a strong or stronger emotional response from your "audience."

Euphemism: Euphemism can be defined as the use of a slightly more mild or indirect term or expression in place of another that might be considered a little bit more harsh, vulgar, or even unpleasant. This can be helpful in softening the blow of a very strong term by phrasing an event or object in more mild terms.

Hyperbole: A hyperbole can be described as a statement that is exaggerated for the purpose of emphasis or even for comedic value. Typically, this type of exaggeration is pushed to an extreme in order to ensure that it is not taken literally. A common example is a statement "I am so hungry I could eat a horse." Obviously, most people could not and definitely would not eat an entire horse. This hyperbole simple serves to illuminate how hungry a person feels.

Irony: Irony can be described as a statement that is used to express a directly opposing meaning or viewpoint in order to help with the expression of the actual point that you are attempting to make. Again, the irony is usually pushed to an extreme much like hyperbole in order to ensure that it is not understood in literal terms.

Juxtaposition: Juxtaposition can be described as the comparing and contrasting of multiple different and sometimes opposing characters, ideas, objects, or events. This is usually used in order to achieve a clearer view of the characteristics or features of one thing by comparing it to those of another one.

Metaphor: Metaphors can be described as the use of non-literal terms in order to describe an action, idea, or object by comparing it to something else. This can be helpful in explaining a thing or an event by associating it with another thing or event that is similar. This can take the form of one thing being described as if it were another, or as a simile. A simile is a type of metaphor that more deliberately states the similarities between two things by saying that "This thing is like that thing," or "This thing is as (adjective) as that thing." The keywords that typically identify a simile are "like" or "as."

Metonym: A metonym is another type of association wherein a word or phrase is replaced with a related word or phrase that acts as a substitute for the real thing. This is normally used for poetic or rhetorical effect. A good example of this type of association is the phrase "The pen is mightier than the sword." This statement describes the power of the written word (which is described here as the "pen") being stronger or potentially having more impact than "the sword," which represents a military force in this context.

Onomatopoeia: Onomatopoeia can be described as a word or group of words that is or are used to represent a sound for the purpose of dramatic or poetic effect, or even realism. This term is used to describe a "word" that describes sounds and usually resembles that sound. Good examples would include things like "Buzz," "boom," "chirp," "creak," or "Sizzle."

Oxymoron: An oxymoron is a combination of two words or terms that, when placed together, are used to express a more dramatic meaning that usually contradicts itself. This is usually used for emphasis or to illustrate a paradox of some sort. This can include phrases like "organized chaos" or "deafening silence."

Chapter 6: Empathy

This chapter will focus on another new skill that can be very helpful in improving your communication skills in a number of different ways. The topic that this chapter will be focusing on will be referred to as "empathy." Empathy can be described as the ability or capacity of one person to relate to and share the emotions, feelings, and point of view of another person or even of a group of people. Empathy can be described as the ability to "step into a person's shoes." This is a little different from the concept of sympathy, which simply describes an understanding or recognition of a person's emotional states or feelings. Empathy goes a little bit deeper than that and is much more useful for effective communication than sympathy is. These differences will be discussed with a little bit more depth later in this chapter, but those are the basic explanations of the two topics. This chapter will specifically be focusing more in empathy than sympathy, however, as this skill is usually a little bit more helpful in connecting with other people and developing better communication skills and improving the quality of your conversations with a person or a group of people, especially ones who may be experiencing particularly strong emotions or who are going through an especially rough experience. This chapter will also go into a little bit more detail about why empathy is usually a little bit more useful for the purpose of developing more effective communication skills. Once you've completed this chapter, you should have all of the tools necessary to master the skills that will be covered in each of the remaining chapters in this section of the book, as well as all of the chapters to be covered in the second section as well.

The next very important skill that will be covered in this section will be very closely related to the topic of "clarity" from the previous chapter, and will be called "empathy." However, this chapter will also discuss sympathy and delve a little bit deeper into the differences between the two, and why that is important.

The first thing that will be discussed is the concept of sympathy. While both sympathy and empathy come from the same root word, the Greek "pathos," which refers to feelings, they are somewhat different concepts. Sympathy can be defined as an understanding of qualities between people or things. The term "sympathy" is usually used to convey feelings of pity or sorrow for someone else, especially someone who is experiencing some sort of misfortune or unpleasant event. It describes a way that a person can feel badly on behalf of another individual, but with a lack of what they are actually feeling or experiencing, or what it is like to be "in their shoes."

Empathy, on the other hand, goes a little bit deeper. Sympathy is a very old word, but the word "empathy" didn't come into existence until centuries later, in the late 19th century. It comes from the same root word as sympathy but is slightly different. Empathy, unlike sympathy, has a very broad meaning. The word "empathy" is typically used to describe the ability or capacity for a person to put themselves in the shoes of another person and imagine the situation that that person is currently experiencing in order to relate to and even experience the feelings, emotions, ideas, or opinions of that person at that moment. Empathy requires a degree of respect for the person who you are empathizing with, and an ability to relate to that person's situation and experiences. Where sympathy is simply the ability to feel compassionate toward a person and to experience sorrow or pity for them and their situation on their behalf, empathy involves actively putting yourself in that person's shoes and relating to how they would be feeling in that situation. In a situation where a friend might be facing a difficult decision or facing an especially unpleasant time, a person who is sympathizing with that person might say something like "I'm sorry, I can imagine how difficult that can be.", while a person who is using the skill of empathy might say something more along the lines of "I understand this is a difficult decision, I experienced something very similar a while back. Would you like some help coming to a decision about it?" This can, of course, be a much better response for the sake of effective communication. Assuring a person that you understand how they feel can help to make them feel much more at ease, and can also help them to calm down and assess the situation a bit more clearly. This can make communication much easier in this situation, allowing for more clarity and a better understanding between you.

Chapter 7: Honesty

This chapter will be about another new skill that is mostly unrelated to the other ones that came before. This chapter's topic will be referred to as "honesty," and will focus on the importance of honesty in order to maintain clear and effective communication. Of course, honesty should not be an unfamiliar concept, so this chapter's focus should not require much of an explanation. However, honesty for the purpose of effective communication goes beyond simply "not lying." In order to communicate clearly and effectively with other people and groups of people, you need to be forthcoming with information such as feelings and emotions that are important to you. The ability to express your thoughts and opinions honestly and completely is a valuable and even vital part of learning to communicate effectively with other people.

Effective and honest communication requires a lot of work to master. Being completely honest about our thoughts, opinions, feelings, and emotions can be difficult for many people, for many different reasons. Some people aren't used to being able to freely express these things and discuss sensitive topics like these. Stating these aspects of your personality can leave you in a very vulnerable and sensitive place, emotionally speaking. The first thing to consider regarding this topic is that effective communication depends largely on mindset. In order to communicate effectively in this way, you need to consider the viewpoints of other people and how they will perceive your words. Another very important aspect of learning how to communicate with others in an effective and honest way is to learn to move past your own defenses and safeguards to vulnerability. Many people are prevented from achieving this goal because of their own insecurities and fears, specifically regarding any sort of emotional vulnerability, real or perceived, that might occur as a result of this kind of honesty. For the sake of becoming a more effective communicator, one needs to learn to move past these fears. The best way to do this is to begin thinking primarily about the person or people that you are communicating with. A conversation should be about the people who you are talking to and with before yourself. This is because when you tell people things, it should be for their benefit, as they are the ones who will be learning this information. Good communication takes a very large amount of hard work to master and maintain. It requires trust and respect, and active attention. Luckily, there are many ways that you can improve your communication skills and learn to become a much more effective and honest conversationalist. These methods will be listed below:

Timing. An important conversation or discussion should not be put off. When important issues arise, they should be handled as soon as possible. Of course, this does not mean that these topics should be discussed or brought up immediately as they come up. Sometimes the situation is awkward or inappropriate. If this is the case, it might be best to handle the issue at a later time when you can discuss the issue in private. Again, though, this does not mean that the issue should be ignored by any means. It is important to handle important problems at an appropriate time. If it's needed, you should even take the time to sort of "cool down" in order to properly discuss this problem. These sorts of things should not be handled when either you or the person you are discussing it with is angry or in a bad mood. That sort of thing can usually lead to escalation or negative results.

Flexibility. Flexibility is a very good quality to have in general, of course. It can also be incredibly important in being a more effective communicator and improving your overall communication skills. Important conversations like the ones that require the kind of honesty that is described in this chapter rarely ever go as planned, and just as rarely go smoothly. These kinds of conversations have ups and downs and often branch out from various tangents or unexpected comments and into similar or related topics that can often turn the conversation into something else, whether good or bad. "Escalation" is a term that many people use to describe the times when these kinds of conversations take a turn that may not be favorable, and this is very easy to fall into in these sorts of complicated situations. For this reason, it can be incredibly important to maintain a sort of flexibility and adaptability. These qualities can help you to quickly recover from an unfavorable situation or to keep a conversation on a good track. A good way to maintain this flexibility is to avoid being rigid when talking about sensitive issues. The more attached you are with a particular outcome, the more disappointed you are likely to become when it doesn't turn out in the way that you expected. As the conversation bends and twists, you should be making an effort to bend and move with it, staying in the moment and in the conversation as it unfolds. The big thing to keep in mind here is acceptance. This conversation might not turn out the way you had expected or hoped it would, and that is okay. Things are what they are. You should always be trying to change the things that you can and accept the things you can't.

Patience. This is another valuable skill, as it can be incredibly important in all aspects of life. Naturally, then, that will also translate to communication. Nobody is perfect, and nobody is capable of conveying their thoughts and feelings with perfect accuracy, especially important ones that can put a good amount of pressure on a person and make them a little bit nervous, which can alter the ways we communicate. Expressing your thoughts and emotions wholly and honestly can be very difficult, and patience is required in these situations in order to allow for an accurate representation of these thoughts and feelings. You should be listening to what this person is saying, and with patience and openness, otherwise, they might feel invalidated or judged, which can lead to negative outcomes like arguments or disagreements, and harm the relationship between that person and yourself.

Acceptance. This is a very similar topic to the second one on this list. Acceptance is incredibly important, again, to keep in mind in most situations, but can specifically be very helpful to communication. Not only should you be accepting of your environment and the situation or situations that you find yourself in, but you should also try to keep an open mindset about the people around you and their feelings or emotions, especially complicated ones that they might have trouble expressing. These kinds of things can be very difficult to talk about for a lot of people and can put us in a place of weakness that makes it difficult to communicate efficiently and effectively. When people feel judged, they can begin to become defensive or even shut down, which can bring a conversation to a halt and prevent honest communication. It is very important to always try to be accepting of the qualities and traits of other people in order to help them feel comfortable about the aspects of themselves that they may feel ashamed of.

Honesty. Of course, the final part of this list will be "honesty." This is very likely the most important part of maintaining effective communication with any other person. You should be forthcoming with your own thoughts and feelings in order to build trust with that person and a positive and open relationship. You shouldn't expect anyone to be honest in this way with you if you aren't also honest with them. You should be forthcoming and communicate well by going to them with important issues and problems as they come up and avoiding deception by not hiding them. Honest and effective communication can be a vital aspect of a good relationship of any kind between two people.

Chapter 8: Respect

Communication can be a very important part of our personal and professional lives, and it is extremely important that we understand how to communicate effectively with other people. However, it can also be very easy for us to forget as well. You should always be keeping these skills in mind and actively trying to use them to help you to communicate with other people, whether they be coworkers, acquaintances, friends, or family. You should always try to practice honest and respectful communication techniques in order to build and maintain positive relationships. Everyone should be allowed to experience their own thoughts and feelings and be able to share those experiences with the people closest to them. Sometimes this is all that a person might need in order to handle a difficult situation. When they need to release some of these feelings or emotions in this way, it is important that they feel accepted and validated, and that they are treated with openness and respect. When talking to a person about experiences, feelings, emotions, thoughts, and ideas that are important to them, it is incredibly important to respect them and their experiences and try to offer support when it is appropriate. While it is definitely possible to gain respect for a person or group of people, however, it might not always be so easy to demonstrate that respect to that person or group of people. Fortunately, there are several ways that you can begin to improve your ability to demonstrate this respect, which will be listed below:

Active listening. In order to maintain effective communication with another person, you should practice "active listening" in order to help that person feel validated and that their concerns, feelings, and emotions are heard and understood. This concept was discussed in the second chapter of this book as well and is an important aspect of respectful and open communication, as well as building and maintaining strong and positive relationships with other people. Active listening involves listening to a person or group of people and giving them your full attention in order to best hear and understand the things that they are saying. You should be using gestures and short phrases to make sure that they know you are paying attention and are interested in what they have to say, while also avoiding distracting or interrupting them. You should also be trying to provide feedback and let them know what you heard and the topic as you understand it so as to avoid or resolve any misunderstandings or miscommunication that might occur before they become larger concerns.

Self-awareness. You should be able to understand how a person's background or their culture can affect the various ways that their personalities and the ways that they will develop. This will apply to both yourself and the people around you. If you understand the various differences between you and the person or people you are communicating with, you can then use that information to better understand where that person or those people are coming from, emotionally speaking. You will also be able to predict that person or those people's reactions and their emotional states, and use that information in order to do things like personalize your words to them and speak in ways that will work best for them. Most misunderstandings or miscommunications between different people occur not as a result of what was specifically said, but the way that it was said. The most effective way to prevent these types of miscommunications is to understand your "audience" and how they will react to the things you are saying.

Honesty and learning. Conversations are not about constantly just agreeing with the other person. You do not need to be a "yes man" and simply try to make a person feel good about themselves or the topic being discussed. They aren't about "winning" either, though. You don't need to disagree with a person and their viewpoints simply for the purpose of creating debate or "winning" the conversation by enforcing your opinion to that person or people. You should, however, be honest about your thoughts, feelings, and opinions. In most cases, there is no right or wrong and you should simply do or say what you think is right. This is a very important part of respect and effective communication. The purpose of being able to communicate with other people is to learn from each other. This can be done more easily by learning to value the opinions, feelings, thoughts, and emotions of other people. By learning to value these aspects of other people around us, especially if they differ from our own possibly opposing aspects of ourselves, we can begin to learn from them and grow more as people. By acknowledging the validity of another person's thoughts and opinions on a particular topic or subject, we can begin to work toward a much more respectful and open relationship with those people and more effective communication with them as well. It might even be possible that someone with directly opposing views or opinions might have the same goals or intentions behind them!

Acceptance. This is very likely the most important part of respectful relationships between people and maintaining honest and healthy relationships with them. You should be accepting of other people, even and especially if they are different from yourself in their opinions and views. This has been discussed in the previous chapter as well and is equally important here. The concept of acceptance is very important to keep in mind in any and all situations that you might find yourself in and can be incredibly helpful for maintaining clear, effective, and respectful communication with other people around you. Not only should you be accepting of your environment and the situation or situations that you find yourself in, but you should also try to keep an open mindset about the people around you and their feelings or emotions, especially complicated ones that they might have trouble expressing. These kinds of things can be very difficult to talk about for a lot of people and can put us in a place of weakness that makes it difficult to communicate efficiently and effectively. When people feel judged, they can begin to become defensive or even shut down, which can bring a conversation to a halt and prevent honest communication. It is very important to always try to be accepting of the qualities and traits of other people in order to help them feel comfortable about the aspects of themselves that they may feel ashamed of.

Boundaries. While not as central to the concept of respect as being accepting of the differences between people, it can also be incredibly important to keep in mind a person's boundaries when talking to them or communicating with them in any way. It can be incredibly important to keep a person's boundaries and limitations in mind, especially if they might be a little bit more sensitive about these boundaries than you might expect. You might be a very social person and don't pay much attention to these little things, but some people might not be as fond as others about things like physical contact or emotional vulnerability and sharing their feelings and emotions. You should be aware of these aspects of each person you are communicating with in order to best communicate with them. In the case of a person who isn't so comfortable with physical contact, you might try to keep a "respectful distance" from them, depending on their comfort zones while also letting them know that you are there for them and expressing the things that you normally would with that sort of physical contact in other ways. If you are talking with someone who is a little bit more emotionally closed off than you are used to, you could try to let them know that you won't judge them and reassure them that you want to help them and are there for them as well. A very important thing that will be useful in these sorts of interactions is time. You should be patient and give these people and their issues the time to adjust and resolve. Otherwise, they might become worse or close themselves off completely to you.

Chapter 9: Criticism

This chapter is about the concept of criticism and how to both offer and accept it well. The concept of criticism is a simple one. Criticism can be described as the expression of an opinion about a person or thing based on the perception of another. This sort of expression is always subjective and dependent on the perception of the person offering it. As such, there are usually feelings involved in it. This can sometimes make it difficult to offer criticism in a healthy way that allows for growth and improvement, as it can often come from strong emotions or feelings, which can alter the ways that we communicate this information to the people it relates to. These strong feelings and emotions can also affect the delivery of another person's criticisms, making it difficult to receive as well. Things like callouts about our personal flaws or negative reactions to things that we may have done can be very hurtful if they are delivered or received in the "wrong" way, or in a way that is a little bit less considerate of our feelings and emotions that we might like. In order to handle these sorts of things, however, it is very important that we learn how to properly both offer and accept criticism, especially about or regarding topics that might be somewhat sensitive. Having the ability to hear and understand the opinions of other people can improve our relationships, performance in work, and our overall emotional health. Luckily, as with most things that seem difficult at first, there are ways to improve and to develop the skills that will allow you to do so in a healthy way. These methods will be separated into three sections; The things or patterns that you should try to avoid, the skills you should work on improving, and how to actually use these skills.

The first group of ways to improve your ability to accept and offer positive and constructive criticism will be focused on the habits that you should try to avoid in everyday life. Before this, though, we should discuss a very specific term that applies to these concepts. This term is called "lashon hara," which translates to "evil tongue." Lashon hara is a Hebrew term which describes a way of speaking about another person or thing in a derogatory or harmful way. Typically, it refers to statements which are technically true, but not meant to be constructive or helpful to a situation. Lashon hara describes statements that are meant only to harm, which is why it is referred to as the "evil tongue." This can involve this sort of negative communication regardless of the medium or media that are used. Lashon hara is a very good example of the type of criticism that should be disregarded or handled with very specific care to avoid justifying and is considered a very serious sin. As was stated before, this is a good example of the type of criticism that should not be validated. There are many times that this is the case with statements meant to criticize, such as statements that are untrue or designed to be harmful to you or the person they are directed toward. This also applies to offer criticism as well. Luckily, however, this is not typically the case, and most of the time when a person offers any sort of criticism, it is actually meant to be helpful. It may be poorly delivered, but usually is meant to be constructive. When we are on the receiving end of critical statements about ourselves, we should be keeping this in mind and trying to use the information provided to learn and grow as people. We should be attempting to benefit from this kind of criticism, and view it through a calm and objective lens in order to use it and develop further as people.

Additionally, when you receive any sort of honest criticism, an instinct that you might have could be to think "oh, this isn't really a big deal. I shouldn't worry about it". It is entirely possible that the issue actually doesn't matter very much to you, as you might not have given the topic much thought. Maybe you will think about it now. But it is obviously important to the person who brought the issue up for discussion and is most likely important for others as well. You should be paying attention to these types of things and trying to use them to improve and grow. You should also be trying to avoid rationalization of the things about yourself that are being criticized. Criticisms should be taken gracefully and used for the sake of improvement. Rationalization of your flaws can be harmful to that improvement and your personal growth. Additionally, if someone is offering you criticism about something you've done, you should try to avoid excuses or justification. When criticized, it is very easy to feel attacked and do this. Instead, you should be asking why it is that these aspects of yourself or the actions you take or have taken are possibly not ideal. You should be facing these criticisms head on and with a positive growth mentality.

Once you have a decent handle on how to understand and accept criticism well, you should move on to learning how to offer it, as well. This should be done with care and attention regarding the feelings and emotions of the people or things you are criticizing. The first thing to keep in mind is to make sure that your criticisms are helpful, and avoid harmful or insulting speech. Another thing to avoid which has already been talked about in this chapter is "lashon hara," as well as any other sort of harmful or unhelpful commentary. Good criticism is used for the purposes of evaluation and judgment and should be offered in order to help people grow and improve. It should never come from a feeling of jealousy or envy, or from your own insecurities about your own situation.

These kinds of comments are not helpful and only serve to hurt yourself and the people around you. In a professional setting, a leader may use constructive criticism in order to point their employees in certain directions and to help them improve the quality of their work. This should not be negative or make those employees upset or uncomfortable around their boss, however. Many people new to leadership positions will tend to be too critical and tell people only what they do wrong without offering advice on how to fix the problem or helping them to understand the problem at all. This is not helpful and will not help other people to improve on those points. Because of this, you should always be trying to make sure that your criticism is helpful and avoid negative or hurtful speech. You should be making an effort to offer criticism that is constructive. Offering thoughtful and helpful feedback can help people to gain extremely valuable insight into our actions, habits, and personality traits. Honest, helpful communication can also help to develop healthy relationships with the people around us and build trust between people as well.

On both sides of criticism, you should be trying to understand and learn from this experience and use it to improve and grow as a person. You should have an "action plan" about how to use this new information to help you move forward. This is very important because many people can tend to lost motivation as a result of certain types of criticism, especially negative or harsh statements. Of course, the first thing you can do to help you handle criticism in the best way is to simply listen. You should be trying to hear and understand the point of what is being said in order to be able to use it afterward. Usually, even if offered in a hostile tone or if meant to be harmful, like in the case of lashon hara, criticism can be helpful as well. You can typically use any sort of criticism to help you grow and develop as a person and learning from the experience. You might be feeling hurt or attacked when someone calls out a specific flaw that you might have, but the knowledge of this flaw can still be used to help you work on improving on things that are affected by this flaw. This leads directly to the next part of this "action plan," which is to respond appropriately. This means that you should react to these criticisms in a calm and respectful way, regardless of the intention of the original statement. You might even decide that you should thank the person who offered this criticism. Always try to "be the bigger person," as they say. A simple smile and a "thank you" can help to diffuse a potentially hostile situation. It can also be incredibly helpful both for yourself and others to view critical statements objectively as opposed to seeing them as attacks on your character. It might also be the case that a specific comment might be directed at a specific action or aspect of your personality or even something you enjoy. This is very important to note as well, as people can sometimes interpret these kinds of statements as if they are about themselves. It can be very important to pay attention to specifically what is being discussed at the current moment.

Chapter 10: Confidence

This final chapter of the first section of this book is a simple concept, but can sometimes be difficult to master. This last skill that will help you in improving your conversational skills and in learning how to communicate much more effectively with other people and groups of people much more effectively is "confidence." Of course, this is most likely a concept that you are familiar with, as it is a fairly common idea. Unfortunately, however, many people confuse it with the concept of pride, which can be harmful to your personal growth and development for reasons that will be discussed in this chapter. This chapter will also discuss various topics related to confidence. This includes the "growth mentality" that was talked about earlier in this book and various topics from the first chapter that are related to the kind of confidence that an emotionally healthy person should have in order to communicate as effectively as possible with the people around them as well as the various ways that you can use to achieve this confidence in order to help yourself grow and improve in your everyday life.

The first thing to discuss is the meaning of the word "pride," and how it differs from confidence. There is a reason that this is considered to be one of the deadly sins, after all. The word "pride" has seemingly taken on a double meaning, being used positively more than negatively. The original use of the word, however, could be used to describe a foolishly or irrationally corrupted and inflated sense of a person's accomplishments, status, or value. With this usage, the word "pride" can be more closely connected with the concept of hubris rather than with confidence. Additionally, pride usually applies to a person's superficial traits or achievements, which can be harmful to our personal growth if we focus on these traits as opposed to ones that will help us in the long run. As was discussed in earlier chapters in this book, a fixation on appearances can serve to "cripple" us and prevent us from taking real steps to improve and grow. Instead of focusing on things like pride and superficial achievements, we should be trying to grow and learn as much as we can at any given moment. This will sort of automatically raise our sense of self-confidence by allowing us to move past our fears and insecurities, and increasing our potential for growth and improvement.

Another good thing to realize is that it is not always about you... In a positive way, of course! Constantly worrying that the "spotlight" is on you and that you are being judged can also force us to focus on our insecurities and stop us from taking action to move forward. This is obviously harmful to us as people and should be avoided. The truth is that, while there are always some exceptions, most people are focused on themselves and are trying to figure out how they should act or behave in any given situation. This might seem like a somewhat contradictory statement, but you should be paying attention to other people and their personalities in order to realize that they are probably not judging you so much as trying to understand the situation and how they should handle that situation. Once you've realized this very important fact, you can then begin to focus on yourself and your own growth instead of trying to avoid judgment from other people. Once you move past this fear of being judged and stop worrying about the opinions of other people, you will be able to begin focusing more on improvement and growth without the burden of those fears.

Additionally, criticisms of ideas that you might have had or actions you might have taken should not be taken as attacks on your character. Most of the time, people will not be ignoring or dismissing the person themselves, but a specific action or thought that that person has taken or had. This is important to note, as you should not be taking these criticisms personally. Viewing these kinds of comments through an objective lens and questioning their actual meeting can be very helpful for the sake of your own self-confidence as well as maintaining calm, rational discussion in any situation. This also applies to interruptions as well. Many people will sort of forget their manners and will tend to interrupt or speak eagerly when they are excited about something, and this can come off as rude or dismissive. Many times, it is not intended this way, and instead is simply a result of that person's excitement about the topic. It is very important not to take this personally as well and to handle the situation accordingly. Understanding the situation and the intention of all of the people that are involved in this situation can affect the way you view this situation and how you view yourself, especially if you have a lack of confidence of any kind. Once you move past this obstacle, you can begin to focus on the things that you are saying and doing, as well as how you say and do these things so that the situation or conversation can proceed as smoothly as possible.

Once you've gained a good sense of confidence in yourself and your abilities, you need to be able to convey that sense of confidence to the people you are talking to. There are a lot of methods that you can use to convey this sense of self-confidence. Things like avoiding the use of the word "just" can help you a lot. Instead of saying something along the lines of "Oh, I just wanted to make sure", or "I was just wondering", which can make you seem unsure about what you are saying and the level of confidence you have about the topic, you could say things like "Out of curiosity", or "Oh, by the way…", which will help to eliminate that feeling of doubt and insecurity about what you have to say. You might even simply remove the "just," as well. Another good method is to state what will work for you in some cases and then ask a question. Something like "I'll be ready in a couple of minutes, will that work for you?" will work well. This can serve to communicate your stance and your own limitations in a confident manner, while also validating those of the people you are talking to by asking about what they need or what they would prefer as well. Other kinds of words and phrases that can prevent the communication of confidence in yourself are "minimizing" phrases, such as "a little" or "a bit." These can serve to minimize the topics and make them seem insignificant when talking about things that are actually important to you and can lead to miscommunication. This can cause a lot of problems and can affect the ways that you communicate with other people. Instead of saying these things, you should be very clear and direct. This will help you to be seen as much more confident, and can also help you to avoid any potential misunderstandings. Along the same line of minimizing misunderstandings and miscommunication, you should be trying to be clear about requests as well. Especially in leadership positions, you should be telling people about things instead of asking. You might want to say something like "Can you get this project finished by the end of the week?" when it needs to be completed by then, you should instead be informing people that this is the case. You might say something more like "I need this to be finished by the end of the week." And then, after that, you might ask "Can you do that?" This will make it much clearer because if you ask, the person who has been given the assignment might not be aware that the project actually needs to be finished by Friday. If you tell them that this is the case and then ask, it changes the request significantly. Not only has that person been informed that their project has a deadline by which it needs to be completed, but they have also been validated by being asked if they can handle that request. This will clear up any confusion about this assignment as well as making sure that it can get done in time. If they say that no, they can't have it done by the end of the week, you might ask for the reason for this, and use that information to come up with a solution to this problem. You might come up with a solution yourself, or ask the person what they think needs to happen, either saying "Again, this needs to be done by the end of the week. How can we make that happen?", or even "Okay, well this project really needs to be finished by the end of the week. I think if we do this, then it could work. What do you think of that?" This will serve to help that person feel validated and possibly less nervous or uncomfortable with their assignment.

Another effective method of helping yourself to be more confident as well as projecting that confidence outward into the world around you is to stop apologizing. Being apologetic like this and constantly saying "I'm sorry" can make other people tend to blame you for those problems, even if they weren't actually your fault or if they weren't originally problems, to begin with. Instead of saying "I'm sorry," you should thank people. This makes them feel appreciated while also eliminating those problems with constant apologies. You should try to turn thanks into a habit that you practice in place of apologies. It can help immensely in most situations and help you to feel and appear as more confident as well.

Section 2: Five Barriers to Effective Communication

Congratulations! You've finished the first section of "How to Raise Successful People: Effective Communication Skills To Handle Difficult People" . That first section of this book went over 10 of the most essential skills that are absolutely necessary to learn in order for you to communicate as effectively as possible with other individuals or groups. These skills are applicable in any and all social encounters that one might find themselves in. They can also be used in conjunction with one or more, or even all of the other skills that are included and discussed in this section of the book. Each of these skills can absolutely be applied alone, and every skill in this section, and the rest of the book as well, will each help you in social encounters and in communicating well with other people or groups.

Each of the topics that are covered in this section are designed to help you communicate more effectively with other people and will help you with this goal in the ways that are specific to each individual topic. Each chapter in this section is meant to help you understand some of the largest hurdles to effective communication, each of which is covered by its own chapter. Each of the five chapters in this section are meant to work well with each of the other topics from their own respective chapters, and even with the chapters from the first section, about the 10 skills that are necessary for effective communication. While all of the skills in this book are designed to help you communicate effectively with others on their own, they can prove to be much more effective when used in combination with all of the other skills that are discussed and explained in this book.

Additionally, this section as a whole has been designed to naturally flow from one skill to the next in a way that will feel organic and will allow for you to understand the concepts that are covered in each individual chapter as easily as possible. Many of the chapters in this section and the concepts and ideas contained within them build on those that are included in previous chapters or are meant to set up for those that will be included in later chapters. The fourth chapter of this section, for example, is about enthusiasm and expressiveness, which can be incredibly helpful in helping you to more accurately convey various concepts and ideas to other people or parties, which will, in turn, help you to communicate with them more effectively both in that moment and in general. This concept of "enthusiasm" expands slightly on the two previous chapters, which were about emotional states, and mannerisms. The second chapter in this section, called "The Emotional States," focuses on specific emotional states and their importance, as well as how these various emotional states can affect the ways that you can communicate with other people. These emotional states and how they affect each individual person can vary greatly and are very important to keep in mind during any sort of attempted communication with other people, especially while you are being affected by strong emotion or emotions. The third chapter in this section, additionally, is called "Mannerisms," and is about the ways that you communicate with other people and how those can affect the ways that you are able to convey to those people the concepts and ideas that you need to. The knowledge gained from these two chapters will be incredibly helpful to you during the fourth chapter, which will build even further on both of the information within these chapters. The chapter on "enthusiasm" will be about exactly what it says; enthusiasm. This chapter will discuss this concept and effective methods of expression, including enthusiasm. This concept will build upon the concepts of the emotional states that one can experience and how they can affect your ability to remain as expressive as you might normally be, as well as how your specific types of mannerisms and the ways that you communicate should affect when and why you should choose to emphasize your points with the application of enthusiasm.

Each of these chapters has been designed to work well with and build off of the previous chapters in this section in a way that flows organically with each of the others in the section, as was stated previously. They are also intended to be read after the first 10 chapters, from the first section of this book, have already been finished. Each section and the chapters within them are specifically designed to be read in the order that they have been placed, in order to help you get the most out of this book as is possible. However, while it is not advised to read these chapters out of order, it is definitely possible. For instance, you may find yourself finishing one chapter and wishing to circle back to another chapter that was covered previously, or even jumping forward to a future chapter and coming back afterward. While this is, as was stated previously, not advised, you may wish to plan your own way through the contents of this book. In the event that this is the case, the chapters in this section will be listed below once again:

- Eye Contact. This chapter will discuss the importance of maintaining eye contact and why neglecting this aspect of communication can be detrimental, as well as how to do so effectively.
- Emotional States. This chapter will be focused on various emotional states and how they can affect the way you communicate with others, as well as how to escape from a negative emotional state or find positive ones.
- Mannerisms. This chapter will be focused on the ways you express yourself and how different mannerisms and forms of expression can act as boundaries or barriers to effective communication.
- Enthusiasm. This chapter will cover the importance of enthusiasm and expressiveness in communicating effectively with others.
- Judgment. This chapter will be about judgment and how it differs from criticism, as well as how it can prevent effective communication between or among people.

Once you've finished each of the five chapters of this section, and learned about five of the largest barriers to communicating in an effective manner, you will have finished the second (and last) section of this book. After you've gone through these two sections and their combined total of the 15 chapters in the book, you should have all of the tools necessary to maximize your potential in social situations and learn how to communicate effectively with other people.

Chapter 11: Eye contact

The first chapter of this section will be about the concept of eye contact and why it can be very important for effective communication, both in positive and negative ways, depending on how it is used. If you don't make eye contact, your words and actions can tend to be perceived as hostile, insensitive, or even deceptive. Of course, this can affect the way that you communicate with other people and the ways that people perceive your intentions. If you are not paying attention to how you look when you talk to other people, you can even give off the wrong vibe or portray the wrong type of emotion or feeling with this eye contact. Luckily, there are a number of "shortcuts," or easier methods that can be used to make sure that you are keeping eye contact and the right kind of eye contact.

One good method that you can use to ensure that you are maintaining eye contact and that will help you to appear as friendly is to use something that is referred to as the "eye color test." This "eye contact test" can help you in any type of personal communication and will help you to appear more confident as well. Whether you happen to be in a relaxed conversation with a friend, at a date, or in a job interview, you can use this method to help you to appear more confident than you are by using this "eye contact test. Additionally, this can help other people feel much more relaxed and like they know you a little bit better. Studies have shown that if you look a person in the eye, you can appear to them as more likable and trustworthy. This very simple and very easy trick can help you to maintain eye contact for a good amount of time to ensure that you will appear as open and trustworthy to the person who you are talking to without accidentally slipping into the "creepy stare." This is why the eye color test is so useful. The goal of this little game is to try to pay attention to people's eye color when you talk to them. When you meet a new person and are interacting with them face to face, whether you have already met them before and know them already or not, you can try to look into their eyes just long enough to notice the color of their eyes. This allows you to make eye contact with that person and achieve the desired goals of connection and establishing trust with a good first impression while avoiding crossing that very thin line into "weird" territory. It's a very simple tool and can be useful if you remember to do it out of habit when you meet someone. This is why it helps to also turn it into a little game with yourself because then you will have a much easier time remembering to do it. You can even use it throughout a conversation as it occurs, as well. If you periodically make eye contact and then break it, it can tell the person you're talking to that you care about what they have to say and about the topic that is being discussed, while still maintaining your position on the correct side of that thin line over to weird. It is also important to make sure that when you look away, you look off to the side, as opposed to down. Looking down can communicate humility or a lack of confidence, and unless this is the desired effect in that particular moment, you should try to avoid doing so.

It can be incredibly important, additionally, to keep in mind that our eyes are designed to be the main form of connecting with the world around us. We rely very heavily on our eyes and they are the primary tool that we use to connect with the people around us, as well. The first sense that we rely on to judge people and objects in our sight, as this is the most easily accessible sense available to us. It is why we judge based on appearances and why visual media is usually the most accessible to us. When a person makes eye contact with us, it attracts our attention and we look over to meet them. Humans are very social as a species, and our eyes are the first thing that we tend to look at in order to connect with other individuals. Our eyes can show a lot of emotion, and have a very wide range. The whites of our eyes allow for other people to very easily be able to see what we are looking at and see when we shift focus to a different object or in a different direction. While many other species will tend to follow the direction that the whole head faces, a human might shift focus to the opposite direction and we are normally inclined to follow the path of the eyes, as opposed to the head as a whole. This emphasis on emotion and on the eyes can be incredibly helpful for social connection and is thought to have helped us to develop cooperative skills in the past, for the sake of survival and civilization.

Because of this, our eyes are very expressive. Our eyes can help us to convey specific thoughts or feelings, as the old saying, "The eyes are the windows to the soul: would suggest. This is also evident in a passive sense, as well. As we grow older, it shows as "crow's feet" in our eyes and wrinkles. If a person is tired or doesn't get enough sleep, they might have bags under their eyes. We can see how focused a person is or if they might be a little bit "zoned out" from their eyes. Whether we intend to or not, we communicate a very large amount of information through our eyes that can be seen by the people around us. When a person is attempting to keep a secret or deceive another person in any way, they may attempt to hide this in our body language and facial expressions, but it very likely still visible in their eyes. This is why many poker players or people attempting to hide their emotions or expressions will typically wear sunglasses in order to hide these features from the people who might see them.

Eye contact can also be used to tell a person that we are paying attention to them and the things that they have to say, and that we are interested in what they are saying as well. Despite the fact that interpersonal connection is more accessible now than ever before, people are still inclined toward more face to face interactions and to know that people are really listening to them. The source of this is the eye contact that we are unable to share through text, and even in video calls. This is a large part of what makes it so difficult for us to convey tone through text because we cannot see the eyes of each other and read their emotions in this way.

Chapter 12: Emotional States

This second barrier on the path to mastering all of the skills necessary for effective communication with other people is emotional states. These can be very important to know about and to keep in mind in order to maintain effective communication. This will involve the ability to be aware of your own feelings and emotional states in order to understand how they affect the ways that you can communicate with other people and how to maintain a favorable emotional state for the sake of your own growth and development and to continue to communicate well with other people, as well as how to understand the emotional states of those other people and how you can use the knowledge of those states in other people to communicate more effectively. If you do not have a good understanding of these emotional states, it can very negatively affect your communication skills and the outcome of different conversations with people. This concept is somewhat related to the concept of mentality from the first chapter, in that it will focus on similar points to the ones that were discussed then, but with regards to emotional states instead of mental ones.

Our feelings and emotions can play a very large role in how we communicate with other people. Emotional awareness can be described as the ability to understand the feelings and emotions of yourself and other people. This can be incredibly helpful to your success and the effectiveness of your communication with the people around you. If you are more or less emotionally aware, you will be able to communicate more or less effectively with those people, as a result. You will be able to see and understand other people's emotional states and to recognize how their emotional states and the way that they feel about a particular person, situation, or topic can affect the ways that they are able to communicate. You can also use this knowledge to gain a better understanding of what those people are actually trying to actually communicate to you and why, especially if they might be in an unusual or abnormal state, mentally or emotionally speaking, that might be affecting their ability to communicate their feelings or thoughts to you. Sometimes, it can even be more important to understand the emotional states that affect the ways that people can communicate as opposed to the words that they are saying directly. For example, if you consider a time that you may have tried to hide a certain feeling or emotion that you were experiencing from another person. It was probably at least a little bit harder than you would have liked. Our emotions show very strongly in our faces and can be very difficult to hide at times, especially with particularly strong ones. Instead of trying to hide your feelings and emotions, or to ignore them, you should try to become more aware of them and those of the people around you in order to help yourself to become a much more effective communicator. Luckily, there are a few methods that you can use to help you to do this. These methods will be listed below:

- Emotional awareness. The first method is to work on becoming more emotionally aware. You can do simple things like pay attention to a person's feelings and the way they express those feelings in order to anticipate their reactions and to understand what they might need in a particular situation. If someone tells you something that seems like it came out of nowhere, you might try to ask yourself why they would tell out that or what led them to say that particular thing to you. People like to use the excuse of "for no reason" for things that they don't immediately understand, but this is rarely, if ever, the case. Most of the time actions or words that a person takes or says that don't seem to have a logical reason simply haven't been explained to you. That person very likely has a reason that makes sense to them, you just don't exactly understand it completely yet. Additionally, these issues can often be very important or seem like a big deal to that person, even if they don't seem that way to you. They might have accomplished a personal goal and be very proud of it, but you might not see it as a big deal. In these situations, it can be very important to recognize this and act accordingly. It might even be the other way around, they tell you something that they don't think is that important or is just said off-handedly, but it matters a lot to you. It can be very important to calmly express that that is important to you without getting angry at that person, especially if they didn't mean to insult you. Understand the intention and motivations of certain people and their actions can help you and them as well in any situation. For this reason, it can be very important to keep these things in mind and to "step into their shoes" to understand these motivations and their emotional states, as well as how they can affect the way your conversation develops as a result.

- It can also be important to do the same for your own emotional states. You should try to be aware of your emotional states and how they affect the ways that you communicate with other people at all times. Again, an issue that is important to you might not seem like such a big deal to another person. Your own feelings and emotions can affect the ways that you communicate with other people just like their emotions can affect them. When you experience a particularly strong feeling or emotion, you should be paying attention to this and why you feel this way. If you are aware of these emotional states, you can then use that knowledge to adjust and make sure that they do not negatively affect your ability to communicate effectively.

- Empathy. This was discussed in the sixth chapter of this book as well but will be very useful to go over again here. Empathy can be described as the ability to understand and relate to the feelings or emotions of another person. This can be incredibly useful for helping you to understand the emotional state of other people, as well as how to handle issues regarding these emotional states. If a person you are talking to is experiencing a particular emotional state, whether it is positive or negative, you can try to understand what exactly they may be feeling, and ask yourself why. Once you understand these emotions, you will also be able to relate to them and understand where they are coming from. This will help you to more effectively handle the situation and to possibly help them to deal with it if that is what they need at that moment. When you are able to relate to a person and their emotional states, you will also be able to better understand how you would want the situation to be handled, or if you would want another person to act or talk in a certain way about the situation.

- Trust. This is another big one that is incredibly helpful for communication. If you do not actively base your relationships and your interactions with other people on trust, it can harm these relationships and interactions a lot. Effective communication requires trust between and among all of the people who are involved in it. If you do not trust a person and the things they say, you can't have a positive relationship with them. It is also important to make sure that you are truthful and honest about your intentions and that you are expressing and communicating your thoughts and feelings to other people. This will make all of your interactions much smoother and will allow all of the people who are involved to know exactly what page they and everyone else are on and will lead to much fewer misunderstandings and miscommunication. It can also be very important to be able to trust your instincts when it comes to reading peoples' emotions and nonverbal cues. If your instincts tell you that something is strange about the way a person is communicating to you, push yourself to look into it. If you don't, you will find yourself questioning the person you're talking to, and you could develop feelings of mistrust for seemingly no reason.

Chapter 13: Mannerisms

This chapter will be about the concept of mannerisms, and how your mannerisms can affect the ways that you are perceived in conversation and in communicating with other people. Mannerisms can be described as any habit or other patterns that you have when you are speaking or communicating with other people. These can take the forms of certain speech tics, gestures like hand movements, or various expressions that you may tend to make a lot.

Every person, regardless of their culture or language, has their own set or sets of mannerisms and a particular manner of speaking that is specific to them that extends to all of the ways that they communicate with other people and groups of people. This can be compared to a specific art style that a cartoonist or painter might have and that people tend to identify their art by. In a very similar way, your speech patterns and gestures can be identified as your own by the people around you, especially people who are familiar with them and with you. Much like how a painter might use a particular style in their art, you use a specific style of mannerisms when you speak, even if you do not realize it. You might say the word "like" a lot in a pause or when you haven't thought before about what you are saying, or you might move your hands around a lot when you speak. Regardless of the specific mannerisms that you have, it is important to know that all of the things you do and the ways that you communicate various ideas, concepts, thoughts, or emotions to other people can have a significant impact on the ways that you are perceived and the ways that your words are perceived by other people and groups of people. Some of the features of your speech and your speech habits may even be considered annoying or odd to another person, and this can change or alter the way that they perceive your words and even the way they perceive you as a person. If you use a particular way of expressing yourself too often, this form of mannerisms might be perceived as such or even viewed as annoying to certain people. Of course, this is very subjective and different mannerisms and aspects of your personality or communication style can be seen as annoying by one person while also being seen as a good thing by another. Your specific style of emoting and your mannerisms are not inherently "bad" traits at all, it's simply a matter of each person's perception of all of your traits and aspects of your personality. There are many different kinds of mannerisms that can be perceived negatively by other people, and these should be used with caution for this reason. Some of these skills that you might wish to look out for will be listed below:

Clearing your throat. Some people tend to clear their throats or cough a lot when they speak, out of anxiety or discomfort. This is, of course, usually unintentional and does not go deeper than that. Usually, people will do this because they are uncomfortable, but it can still be perceived as annoying or somewhat distracting to the people they are talking to. This should be kept in mind when you are talking to other people as it can be important to avoid depending on the person.

Specific speech patterns. Some people will say specific words or phrases a lot, and this can detract from the point of their actual words in some cases. Again, it is usually not intentional, but some people can tend to find it somewhat distracting. This includes things such as saying "like" a lot, as well as starting your sentences with "listen," or "you know."

Non-verbal communication habits. Some people also have specific non-verbal habits that they use a lot and even too much, in some cases in conversation. These habits can be seen more as off-putting or even weird or creepy, as opposed to simply annoying. This can include certain behaviors like excessively strong or prolonged eye contact, which can often be perceived as creepy and overly intense by some people. Additionally, there are other behaviors that should be paid attention to, like crossing your arms, which can be perceived as defensive or make you seem uncomfortable with a person or situation. Shifting a lot when you are talking to people can also make you seem uncomfortable and can be very distracting and worrying for the people who you are talking to, as well. It may even be the case that "talking with your hands" can be distracting to some people if they are not used to this sort of expression, and using stimulating behaviors or "fidgeting" with objects around you can be very distracting as well. Other behaviors can be very helpful, like nodding when people are talking to show them that you are paying attention to what they are talking about can also be helpful.

Stance. Some people might tend to shift their stance a lot or stand on one foot at a time. This can convey a sense of unease or discomfort and can make the person you are talking to feel anxious themselves. One example of this is that some people might wrap one leg around the other when they are standing or sitting. This can communicate a sort of shyness to the other person or even to a group of people, which can also make them feel anxious or like they are inconveniencing you. It can also make you somewhat unstable and can cause you to sway to the side, which can also be somewhat distracting. Another example is when people will turn their feet so that they are balancing at a weird place on their feet, like their toes or their heels, and even on the sides of their feet. This can convey a sense of discomfort, much like many of the other examples in this list, or even reveal feelings of awkwardness or embarrassment to the people they are talking to.

Posture. Your posture can also communicate different things and different emotions to the people who you are talking to. Holding stances such as leaning on a chair, table, or stand can convey an attitude that is often inappropriately casual, or even a little bit too familiar, in some cases. In some cases, like presentations in a workplace, taking this "dying warrior" stance can even make you seem lazy or exhausted, which can communicate a lack of professionality to your "audience."

Fidgeting. This sort of behavior can communicate to your "audience" that you are distracted, or wanting to remove yourself from the situation. Actions such as putting your hands in your pockets and pulling them out a lot, or looking at your wrist or watch too often can tell your "audience" that you do not want to be there with them. It also conveys a sense of anxiety and nervousness, as well. This can, in turn, make the people who you are talking to feel nervous or anxious as well, or even a little bit disrespected, which is never ideal.

Nodding a lot. This is another kind of communication that people use a lot more than they may realize in everyday conversation. Usually, this form of expression is combined with other forms, like short words of encouragement like "yeah" or "uh-huh." If a person is nodding a lot when you are talking to them, it might be a sign that they aren't as interested in the current topic as you are. They might be trying to be polite and let you talk about the situation out of kindness. This doesn't necessarily mean that they are completely uninterested or that they don't actually want to be talking to you, however. It might be the case that even though this person is a friend and enjoys talking to you, they are focused on other things at the moment or simply aren't as interested in what you are talking about, but that they still know that you are interested and want to let you express that interest. Regardless of the reason for this behavior, if this is the case, it might be time to switch over to a new topic of discussion.

Chapter 14: Enthusiasm

This chapter will be about the concept of enthusiasm and how enthusiasm can be an important aspect of effective communication with other people. It can affect the ways that you communicate with these people and how they perceive your words and intentions. Enthusiasm is a very important skill to master and can be incredibly helpful for effective communication. This chapter will be somewhat related to the chapter from the first section of this book, which was about confidence. Confidence and enthusiasm come hand in hand, and mastering one will help with the other, and both will help you to learn to communicate much more effectively with other people. There are a number of useful tricks that you can use to help you communicate more effectively in this way, however.

As was discussed in the chapter of this book about confidence, this can be a somewhat difficult skill to master. The skill of confidence can help you in improving your conversational skills and in learning how to communicate much more effectively with other people and groups of people. However, as long as you are focused primarily on the idea of "being confident," you are focused on yourself. This chapter will be more about shifting your focus over to other people. When you focus your attention on a person or a thing that is important too, whether it be your work, a friend or romantic partner, or even a hobby that is particularly important to you, you will become more energized and enthusiastic about that topic, which can help other people to become invested in the things that you have to say as well. When you are more emotive and more interested in something, other people are much more likely to become invested in it as well.

You should also try to think about the people who you are speaking to and how they will interpret the things that you say to them and their experience during this conversation. You should be asking yourself how your concepts and ideas are being interpreted by the people you are talking to. How are they reacting to this topic or topics? Are they interested in it themselves, or do they even understand it or why you are interested? If they don't seem to be invested in the topics personally, what can you do to help them to become invested? If they are giving you any sort of feedback, like nods or asking questions, maybe you can use this information to make it easier for them to understand where you are coming from. This might help them to enjoy it more and might cause them to share a little bit of your enthusiasm. If you communicate your point and the reasons why you are interested and enthusiastic about a particular topic, it can be very easy for other people to become invested in that topic as well. We can connect with other people because of the things that we like, but the real reason behind this is that different people can often share the same reasons for liking something and feeling enthusiastic about it. When you keep this in mind and use it to appeal to different people who might also share those reasons, your enthusiasm can become almost infectious. Communicating your enthusiasm with other people can be difficult. However, there are a number of ways to communicate enthusiasm to other people, which will be listed below:

Actively emote. You should make an active effort to be enthusiastic about everything that you do and say. Add a little bit of "color" to your words and actions and communicate a little bit more enthusiasm or excitement to other people. If you make an effort to smile, greet people enthusiastically, or lighten your expression a little bit, other people will be much more receptive to you and the things that you are talking about. If you use more colorful and descriptive words to describe things that you are passionate about and vary your tone, that passion will become apparent to other people as well. Emphasize verbs and adjectives, and don't be afraid to convey your passion about these topics. If you make the conversation livelier, you will feel it, and the people you are talking to will feel it as well. You might even gesture with your hands or move around when you talk. Making sure to perform small acts like this can help people to share your sense of enthusiasm about the things that you are talking about.

Share your opinions with other people without forcing them onto those people. You should try to express your opinions to other people when you are passionate and enthusiastic about something. They should be allowed to form their own opinions about the subject, but it can also be helpful if you explain the topic to them and why you feel so strongly about it. The key with this is to be passionate when discussing your feelings about the subject, while also talking about the actual topic objectively. You should try to be accurate and informative about the topic and avoid letting your own feelings about it, whether those feelings are positive or negative, affect the way you explain it. You can still speak passionately about these aspects of the things that you are talking about, of course, but in a way that lets other people form their own opinions and know that it is still okay if they aren't as interested as you are.

Practice positivity. You should be trying to spread praise as much as you can. If you express your appreciation of people, this will make them, of course, feel appreciated. You should try to be warm, kind, and sincere to people and compliment them for the things that they do, whether those things benefit you or not. You should always try to spread positivity at all times. If you make people feel appreciated and share your enthusiasm and praise with them, this can also help them to share your passion without even expressing to them why you feel this way yourself. Additionally, you should always try to look for the good in the people around you and in various situations, especially in ones that don't immediately seem positive to you. You should walk away from gossip or malicious actions, and instead focus on positivity. This can help other people to share your passion and enthusiasm.

Make other people feel valued and important. Effective communication is all about the people you are talking to. This can be said about any situation that involves communicating with other people but applies even more to specific times when you are especially enthusiastic or excited about a particular topic or situation. It is important to pay attention to the feelings and emotions of other people, otherwise, your words might be misunderstood or completely fly over the heads of other people. Make others feel important - In the necessity to satisfy a universal craving the necessity to make others feel important. At the end of the day, this is the main thing that most people want. People like to feel important and wanted, and talking to them about things that you are excited about can be helpful for this reason. You can show other people that they are important to you by expressing your enthusiasm to them and by going to them about topics or situations that you are enthusiastic about. Of course, however, this attention should be defined clearly. You should plan it, to a slight degree. You will need to talk to this person in clear terms that this person will be able to understand.

Pay attention to the feelings and emotions of other people. When you are very excited or enthusiastic about something, it can be much easier for you to forget this. You will be much more likely, in this case, to accidentally say something insensitive or rude that can put other people off. For this reason, you should also try to be careful about the things that you say and try to plan out your words and your actions as much as possible. You can do this by looking out for specific mannerisms that different people exhibit when you are talking to them. This topic was discussed in the previous chapter as well. The types of mannerisms that can be important to look out for in these kinds of situations include things like a person's stance, posture, and other forms of non-verbal communication. If a person is fidgeting a lot, they are probably uncomfortable or anxious. If this is the case, it might be time to switch to a different topic or to keep your enthusiasm in check a little bit more. This also applies to other types of behaviors, such as shifting stance or nodding a lot. If a person is nodding a lot when you are talking to them, it might be a sign that they aren't as interested in the current topic as you are. They might be trying to be polite and let you talk about the situation out of kindness. This doesn't necessarily mean that they are completely uninterested or that they don't actually want to be talking to you, however. It might be the case that even though this person is a friend and enjoys talking to you, they are focused on other things at the moment or simply aren't as interested in what you are talking about, but that they still know that you are interested and want to let you express that interest. Regardless of the reason for this behavior, if this is the case, it might be time to switch over to a new topic of discussion.

Chapter 15: Judgment

This chapter will be about the concept of judgment and how it can be a very significant obstacle to effective communication with other people. It can affect the ways that you communicate with these people and how they perceive your words and intentions. It can be very easy to slip into a sort of "judgmental" and negative frame of mind. Of course, that sort of negativity is less than ideal, as a state of mind to possess, for obvious reasons. If you practice "mindful communication," you can practice the act of paying attention to your words and the ways that they will affect the people who you are talking to at any given moment. The essence of this type of communication is observation, as opposed to evaluation. Many people will tend to deal with unfamiliarity by assessing things or situations, which can be perceived as negative or overly critical. Avoiding becoming judgmental and having a negative mindset can be very difficult at times. Fortunately, however, there are a number of ways that people can avoid falling into this kind of mentality. These methods will be listed below:

Pay attention to your reactions and the things that you say. If you can begin to pay attention to the things that you say and your reactions to different people, things, and situations, then you can also change them if they happen to be negative or too judgmental. By being conscious of our habits in conversation, we can identify the not so good aspects of the ways that we communicate and we can then use that information to learn and grow from them in order to develop a much more positive mindset. It can be very easy for us to forget to maintain a positive outlook that focuses on growth and improvement, as was mentioned in the first chapter of this book on mentality. Along without words and reactions to various things, it is also very important that we pay attention to our thoughts and feelings, especially in difficult or uncomfortable situations. It is very important for us to take the time to recognize and acknowledge our reactions, thoughts, and feelings too difficult or uncomfortable situations objectively and in a calm manner. If you slow down when you are uncomfortable in these types of situations, it can make it much easier to do this. You might take a few seconds or take a deep breath, or use any other method you may have to help you to cope with stressful situations. This can help you to view the situation as objectively as possible, as well.

Actively avoid judgmental tendencies. When we begin to pay attention to people, things, and situations around us, we can tend to resort to judgment about them, almost as a reflex. Phrases or thoughts that are meant to evaluate or assess these things might seem harmless to you might matter a lot to someone else, and are the kinds of statements that should be avoided. We should be actively trying to help others and ourselves suffer less, and criticizing or judging these kinds of things will only make everyone involved suffer more. Mindful communication involves doing things like actively trying to stop viewing things in terms of right or wrong and good or bad. You should be trying to stop seeing these things as better than or less than, but simply as they are, independently of anything that they might be compared to for the sake of judgment or evaluation. This can be accomplished easily if you make an effort to avoid this kind of judgment and to stop "gossiping" about or evaluating others. A big thing to consider is that everyone is the same. Our circumstances are the only things that separate us and our lives as people. Without these differences in our personal stories, people are essentially the same. If you are able to keep this sameness in mind, it can be much easier for us to understand the differences between us and other people. If you happen to be judging yourself, it is very important that you also let yourself feel and experience that without letting it take over or becoming too critical of your behaviors and habits. Instead, you might stop to take note of this feeling and take the opportunity to learn and grow from it, and then you will be able to let that thought go and move forward.

Make sure to "be in the moment." It can be very important for us as people to keep our thoughts on the present at all times. You are allowed to use events to help you grow, but you should always primarily be trying to improve and grow at all times. It is very easy for us to slip into a state of mind that is focused on events that happened in the past, or that needs to be done in the future. This can be bad, as it can distract us from the present and diminish the importance of what is happening around us. Additionally, being focused too much on the past or on the future can make it much easier to slip into "toxic" habits, and to become too judgmental of ourselves and the people around us.

Conclusion

Congratulations! Once you have finished all fifteen chapters of "How to Raise Successful People: Effective Communication Skills To Handle Difficult People", you should have all of the tools that you need in order to do just that: improve your conversations and communication skills as effectively as possible by focusing on the essential skills that you will need in order to effectively navigate your way through any and all social encounters you might experience. You can also use this information in order to grow and develop as a person, moving forward, as well as maximizing your potential in conversation with other people. The first section of this book went over ten very important skills to help you to understand how to communicate as effectively as possible and how to put these skills into practice in your everyday life, starting with the type of mentality that you will need for effective communication and how you can put yourself in the right frame of mind for you and your own personal growth and improvement as a person.

The second section of this book made a bit of a shift in focus, switching over to five more skills that you can learn to understand and master that, if poorly understood or ignores, can act as obstacles in the road to mastering your communication skills and becoming a more effective conversationalist.

This can be a very difficult, time-consuming, and mentally exhausting task, but this book is designed to help you in this goal of improving your conversations and communication skills as effectively as possible by focusing on the essential skills that you will need in order to effectively navigate your way through any and all social encounters you might experience by acting as a guide in helping you to use the information within this book in order to grow and develop as a person, moving forward, as well as maximizing your potential in conversation with other people.

Made in the USA
Coppell, TX
04 November 2019